IMAGES

Winter

Karen Bryant-Mole

Heinemann

First published in Great Britain by Heinemann Library, Halley Court, Jordan Hill, Oxford OX2 8EJ,
a division of Reed Educational & Professional Publishing Ltd.

OXFORD FLORENCE PRAGUE MADRID ATHENS MELBOURNE AUCKLAND KUALA LUMPUR
SINGAPORE TOKYO IBADAN NAIROBI KAMPALA JOHANNESBURG GABORONE
PORTSMOUTH NH (USA) CHICAGO MEXICO CITY SAO PAULO

Designed by Jean Wheeler
Commissioned photography by Zul Mukhida
Printed in Hong Kong

01 00 99 98 97
10 9 8 7 6 5 4 3 2 1

ISBN 0 431 06297 8

British Library Cataloguing in Publication Data
Bryant-Mole, Karen
Winter. - (Images)
1.Winter - Juvenile literature
I.Title
508

**Some of the more difficult words in this book are
explained in the glossary.**

Acknowledgements
The Publishers would like to thank the following for permission to reproduce photographs. Cephas; 6 (right) Mike
Herringshaw, Chapel Studios; 19 (right) Graham Horner, Eye Ubiquitous; 11 (left) D Gill, Oxford Scientific Films; 7 (left)
Arthur Butler, 14 (left) Claude Sifelman, 15 (left) Chris Sharp, Positive Images; 6 (left), Tony Stone Images; 7 (left) Darrell
Gulin, 10 (left) Bob Torrez, (right) Colin Raw, 11 (right) David R Frazier, 14 (right) J F Preedy, 15 (right) Natalie Fobes,
22 (left) Mike Timo, 22 and 23 (both right), Mark Junak, 23 (left) Hiroyuki Matsumoto, Zefa; 18 (left), 19 (left)

Every effort has been made to contact copyright holders of any material reproduced in this book. Any omissions will be
rectified in subsequent printings if notice is given to the Publisher.

Contents

Vegetables

sprouts

leeks

turnips

swede

celery

What's your favourite
winter vegetable?

5

Flowers

Even in winter, there are flowers in bloom.

Bed-time

These things keep you cosy at bed-time.

a hot water bottle in a cover

a soft toy

slippers

Snow

in the country

in the forest

on the road

in the park

Clothes

These clothes will keep you warm on a chilly day.

Animals

Some animals rest through the cold winter months.

black bear

dormouse

snow geese

caribou

Some travel to
warmer countries.

Indoor games

What do you like to do when it's too cold to play outside?

Festivals

Here are some festivals that take place during the winter.

Chinese New Year

Hanukkah

Christmas

Mardi Gras

Decorations

These decorations could be used
to decorate a Christmas tree.

Sports

Have you tried any of these winter sports?

Glossary

bloom when flowers open out
caribou wild reindeer
dormouse a small mouse that looks rather like
   a squirrel

Index